# The Amazon River

### By Mary Schulte

**Subject Consultant**
Dr. Cecil Keen
Professor of Atmospheric Sciences/Geography
Minnesota State University, Mankato, Minnesota

**Reading Consultant**
Cecilia Minden-Cupp, PhD
Former Director of the Language and Literacy Program
Harvard Graduate School of Education
Cambridge, Massachusetts

Un⎸ Library

Children's Press®
A Division of Scholastic Inc.
New York   Toronto   London   Auckland   Sydney
Mexico City   New Delhi   Hong Kong
Danbury, Connecticut

Designer: Herman Adler Design
Photo Researcher: Caroline Anderson
The photo on the cover shows the Amazon River's Anavilhanas Archipelago.

**Library of Congress Cataloging-in-Publication Data**

Schulte, Mary, 1958–
  The Amazon River / by Mary Schulte.
      p. cm. — (Rookie read-about geography)
  Includes index.
  ISBN 0-516-25031-0 (lib. bdg.)          0-516-29700-7 (pbk.)
  1. Amazon River—Juvenile literature. I. Title. II. Series.
  F2546.S38 2006
  918.1'1'02—dc22                                              2005021249

JE
SC H
c. 1          7/06

CHILDREN'S PRESS, and ROOKIE READ-ABOUT®,
and associated logos are trademarks and/or registered trademarks
of Scholastic Library Publishing. SCHOLASTIC and associated logos
are trademarks and/or registered trademarks of Scholastic Inc.

1 2 3 4 5 6 7 8 9 10 R 15 14 13 12 11 10 09 08 07 06

The mighty Amazon River begins as a tiny stream in Peru. Peru is a country in South America.

Water into the Amazon River comes from many sources. Snow melts. Rain falls. Streams join the flow. The river grows bigger and faster.

The Amazon River finally rushes into the Atlantic Ocean. Millions of gallons of water pour into the ocean *per second*.

These surfers are riding waves on the Amazon River where it meets the Atlantic Ocean.

The Amazon River is one of the longest rivers on Earth. It measures about 4,000 miles (6,400 kilometers).

It is also the widest river. In some places, you can stand on one side and not see the opposite shore.

The Amazon contains more water than any other river. It holds more than the Mississippi, Nile, and Yangtze rivers put together.

A statue of Francisco de Orellana

In 1541, Spanish explorer Francisco de Orellana met a tribe of fierce women in South America. He and his men fought the women near the river.

The tribe reminded de Orellana of ancient Greek women warriors called Amazons. De Orellana named the river after them.

The Amazon River and
its tributaries flow through
Peru, Bolivia, Venezuela,
Colombia, Ecuador,
and Brazil.

Tributaries are smaller
rivers and streams that
flow into a bigger river.

VENEZUELA

*Atlantic Ocean*

COLOMBIA

*Equator*

**Amazon River**

ECUADOR

*Amazon River Basin*

*Amazon Rain Forest*

PERU

BRAZIL

North
West ✦ East
South

BOLIVIA

SCALE 1 inch = 500 miles

0        Miles        500

0     Kilometers     800

A basin is the land drained by a river and its tributaries. The Amazon River basin covers almost half of Brazil.

When rain falls, it flows to the lowest point in the basin. The lowest point is the Amazon River.

The Amazon River is on the equator. The equator is the midline of the Earth.

More than 400 inches (10 meters) of rain fall near the equator each year. This area is warm and humid. It is tropical.

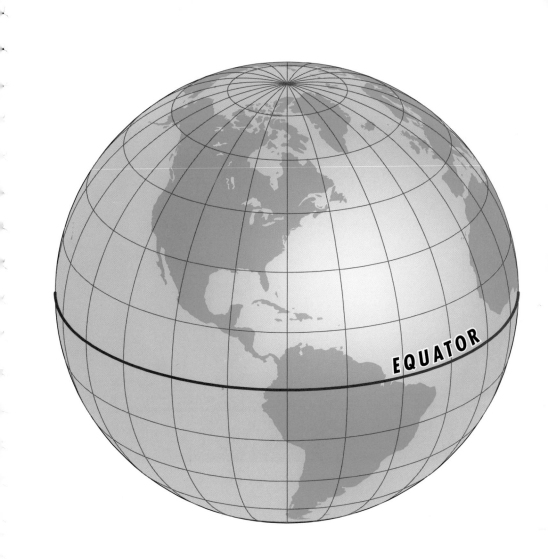

EQUATOR

17

Tropical rain forests exist around the equator. The Amazon River is part of the largest rain forest in the world.

Amazing animals live in the Amazon.

The anaconda is the biggest snake in the world. It slithers in the river's shallow waters.

Anacondas are constrictors. Constrictors coil around their prey and crush them.

One of the world's largest freshwater fish swims in the Amazon. The pirarucu can weigh more than 400 pounds (181 kilograms).

Razor-toothed piranhas also prowl the Amazon. They travel in schools of about twenty fish. Piranhas attack when they smell blood.

Pink river dolphins called
boto play in the river.
Boto have long, thin beaks.

Native people called Amerindians live in the Amazon basin.

They get most of their food from the Amazon River. They travel on the Amazon in canoes. They depend on the river to survive.

Maybe one day you'll visit the Amazon River!

# Words You Know

Amerindians

anaconda

boto

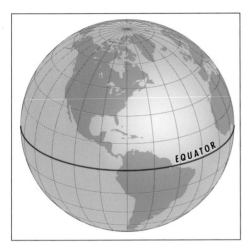

equator

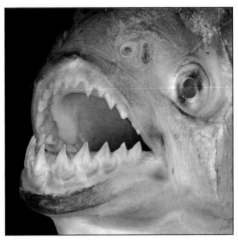

piranhas

rain forest

31

# Index

## About the Author

Mary Schulte is a newspaper photo editor and author of books and articles
for children. She enjoys writing for children and hopes to do the photography
for her books someday. She has written one other book in the Rookie Read-
About® Geography series. She lives and works in Kansas City, Missouri.

## Photo Credits

Photographs © 2006: AP/Wide World Photos/Enrico Marone: 5, 31 top left;
Buddy Mays/Travel Stock: 26; Corbis Images/Royalty-Free: 9; Danita Delimont
Stock Photography/Gavriel Jecan: 6; Mauricio Bianchi/www.andinautas.com.ar: 3;
Minden Pictures/Frans Lanting: 18, 31 bottom; National Geographic Image
Collection/Paul Zahl: 23, 31 top right; Nature Picture Library Ltd./Todd Pusser:
25, 30 bottom; NHPA/Martin Wendler: 21, 30 top right; Peter Arnold Inc./
Luiz C. Marigo: 22; South American Pictures: 29 (Sue Mann), 10 (Tony Morrison);
Superstock, Inc./age fotostock: cover; TRIP Photo Library/Jane Sweeney: 14.

Maps by Bob Italiano